Revised Edition

Happy Cooking and good health Judy Ladergne Riley, 1985

The Soy of Cooking

A Tofu and Tempeh Recipe Book

by Reggi Norton and Martha Wagner
graphics by Reggi Norton

WHITE CRANE PUBLICATIONS

Additional Copies may be ordered for $3.95 plus $1.00 postage and handling from:

WHITE CRANE, P.O. Box 3081, Eugene, OR 97403 or
P.O. Box 56230, Washington, D.C. 20011
(Washington, D.C. residents add sales tax)

Make checks payable to WHITE CRANE.
Please inquire for wholesale prices.

Typography: Amy de Boinville, Illustrations Unlimited,
Silver Spring, Maryland

Printing: Fairfield Graphics, Fairfield, Pennsylvania

ISBN 0-9604880-2-2

Published by WHITE CRANE, P.O. Box 3081, Eugene, OR 97403

Preface

Tofu, protein staple of East Asia for many centuries, and tempeh, Indonesia's most popular soy protein food, may be America's most talked about foods of the Eighties. These two high protein foods made from soybeans offer healthy alternatives to the typical American diet. They are low in saturated fat, low in calories, and free of cholesterol and preservatives.

You don't have to be a vegetarian or a dieter to enjoy tofu and tempeh, and you don't have to be an accomplished oriental cook. These versatile and convenient-to-use foods can be quickly transformed into a limitless array of tasty and familiar dishes — from mayonnaise to burgers, lasagna to cheesecake.

We offer this expanded and revised edition of *The Soy of Cooking* to help you experience the versatility of tofu and tempeh. We hope your palates will be delightfully surprised with the joys of soy!

And thank you to the many friends who have tried our "trial recipes" time and again and who have supported us in other ways with each edition. We love you.

We like to serve certain favorite recipes to people new to the delights of tofu and tempeh. You might want to try these recipes, listed below, first:

"Nearly Chicken" Tempeh Salad

Tofu Mayonnaise

Spicy Tofu Pate

Down Home Corncakes

Barbecued Tempeh

Savory Tofu Pie

Baked Marinated Tofu

Tofu Cheesecake

Pumpkin Pie

Tofu Creme

Table of Contents

Introduction 1

Tofu and Tempeh Basics 4

Salads, Dressings, and Dips 5

Sunny Tofu Salad 5
"Nearly Chicken" Tempeh Salad 6
    "Nearly Tuna," Dilly and Curried Variations 6
Marinated Tofu Cubes 7
Cottage Tofu Spread 7
Tofu Mayonnaise 8
Tofu Tartar Sauce 9
Tofu Sour Cream 9
Tofu Tahini Dressing 10
Lemon Poppy Dressing 10
Tofu Russian Dressing 11
Tofu Mustard Dip 12
Garlic Dill Dip/Dressing 12
Deviled Tempeh Dip/Spread 13
Marinated Steamed Tempeh 13
Tofu Cucumber Raita 14
Creamy Curry Dip 14

Light Meals and Snacks
including appetizers and soups 15

Tofu Rice Burgers 15
Tempeh Burger or "TL&T" 16
Down Home Corncakes 17
Spicy Tofu Pate 18
    Spicy Soy Patties 19
    No-Meat Balls 19
    Pizza Topping 19
Tofu Jerky 20
Stir-Fried Tofu 21
Scrambled Tofu 22
Deep-Fried Tempeh 23
Shallow-Fried Tempeh 23
Avocado Tofu Spread 24
Peanutty Tofu Spread 24

More Light Meals and Snacks...

Soups with Soy 25
Miso-Tofu Soup 25
Fruity Crepes 26
Spinach Crepes 27
Walnut Balls
    with Tofu Lemon Cream Sauce 28

Main Courses 29

Tempeh Shish Kebabs 29
Tofu Moussaka 30
Lasagna 32
Barbecued Tempeh 34
Tempeh "Sloppy Joes" 35
Tempeh or Tofu Burritos 36
Tempeh or Tofu with Sesame Miso Sauce 37
Savory Tofu Pie 38
Baked Marinated Tofu 40
    Tofu Cutlets with Mushroom Gravy 40
    Everyday Tofu 40
Creamed Spinach 41
Spinach Noodle Casserole 41
Hearty Stew with Corn Dumplings 42
Groundnut Stew 44
Curried Tempeh or Tofu 45

Desserts and Muffins 47

Tofu Cheesecake 47
Pumpkin Pie 48
Tofu Creme 49
Peach Tofu Pie 50
Carob Tofu Pie 51
Pastry Crusts 52
Tofu Rice Pudding 53
Tofu Banana Pudding 54
Tofu Peanut Cookies 55
Tofu Herb Muffins 56
Creme Puffs a la Tofu 57

Introduction

Get acquainted with the soybean family and some ingredients which may be new to you.

SOYBEANS are the most nutritious of beans and the only legume which offers complete protein, containing all eight essential amino acids. They have a higher percentage of protein by weight than most foods, 34 percent as compared to 15-20 percent for meats. Domesticated in Asia, where they have been the major protein source for thousands of years, soybeans are now the U.S. number one cash crop, providing the primary source of livestock feed. They can produce more protein per acre than any other grain, legume, or animal. Twenty soy eaters can be fed from the land it takes to feed one meat eater. If the worldwide soybean production were used to feed people rather than animals it could meet more than a third of the world population's protein needs. Definitely food for thought......

TOFU, also known as soybean curd, was first made in China more than 2000 years ago. It is made from soybeans, water and a curdling agent in a process similar to making dairy cheese. The beans are ground and cooked with water, the bean hulls are filtered out, and the remaining "soymilk" is curdled with a coagulant (either calcium sulfate or nigari, a sea water extract). In the final step, the curds are pressed into firm blocks.

Tofu, as you will see, is more versatile than whole soybeans. Its very blandness makes it possible for cooks to turn tofu into "the food of 10,000 flavors." It is also easier to digest than whole soybeans. An ideal diet food, ounce for ounce tofu has about one-third the calories of eggs and one-fourth the calories of beef. An 8-ounce serving of tofu can supply a quarter to half of your daily protein requirements. As a plant food, tofu is cholesterol-free. It is also low in saturated fats, low in sodium (one-fifth the sodium of hamburger or yogurt, one-thirtieth the sodium of cottage cheese), and rich in minerals, especially potassium, iron and calcium. Tofu is also good for your pocketbook, generally less than $1 per pound.

4 ounces tofu = 74 calories, 9 grams protein, 4.7 grams fat, 2.3 grams carbohydrate, 54-150 mg. calcium, 2 grams iron, and 8 mg. sodium.

TEMPEH (TEM-pay), a traditional Indonesian soyfood, is a white, chewy-textured cake of soybeans (or other beans or grains) bound together by a mold culture. Like miso and yogurt, it derives special nutritional benefits from the fermentation process. This 24-hour process endows tempeh with vitamin B-12 (a necessary vitamin available in very few plant foods) and makes it more easily digestible than whole beans. Unlike tofu, tempeh uses the whole bean, making it a good source of fiber as well.

4 ounces tempeh = 170 calories, 17 grams protein, 6 grams fat, 13 grams carbohydrate, 142 mg. calcium, and 5 mg. iron.

SHOYU (SHO-yu), is Japanese-style soy sauce, made from soybeans, cracked roasted wheat, salt, water and a fermentation starter. It is sold at most natural food stores, sometimes as "tamari," which is actually a wheat-free Japanese soy sauce. Both products are superior to most of the American-made soy sauces, which commonly contain food coloring, corn syrup and preservatives.

MISO (MEE-so) is a fermented soybean paste, a staple of China and Japan, used as a seasoning in soups, spreads, salad dressings, and other dishes. Miso is made from soybeans, salt, water, a starter culture (Koji) and usually a grain (rice or barley). As with other fermented foods, its healthful microorganisms aid digestion and, so the Japanese believe, promote good health and long life; they have a proverb that a bowl of miso soup each day keeps the doctor away! High heat destroys miso's valuable enzymes, so add it at the end of cooking. It is a protein booster when eaten with grains or breads. Varieties range from dark to light, salty to sweet. From the salty and heartiest to the lightest and sweetest are: hatcho, mugi, genmai, kome, light yellow, red, white.

2

SOYMILK, prepared from dried soybeans, can replace cow's milk in cooking and as a beverage. It is lower in calories and fat than cow's milk, nearly as high in protein, and may be enriched to provide as much calcium as cow's milk. Powdered soymilks are also available but lack the good flavor of fresh soymilk. Some excellent soymilk ice creams are now being produced using high-quality natural ingredients. They are less rich than dairy ice creams and a real treat for the non-dairy eater.

TAHINI is a smooth, creamy paste of unroasted or lightly roasted hulled sesame seeds. Sesame butter, made from unhulled roasted sesame seeds, has a stronger flavor than tahini. Popular in the Middle East, tahini is available in supermarket specialty or natural food sections and in most natural food stores. Small amounts lend richness to sauces, dressings, spreads, desserts, and main dishes. Sesame seeds are a good source of protein and calcium; they can be ground to a fine meal in a blender.

GOMASHIO (go-MAH-shi-oh) is a seasoning made by mixing roasted, ground sesame seeds and salt and/or kelp to taste, usually in a ratio of 6:1 or 8:1; this is one way of cutting down on salt.

We tend, by the way, to put little salt, shoyu, or miso in most recipes and recommend that you eliminate these from the recipes altogether if you are on a salt-restricted diet.

NUTRITIONAL YEAST, sometimes known as Brewer's Yeast, is a food supplement available at most natural food stores. It does not have rising properties like baking yeast. It is a good source of protein and B vitamins. Available in powder or flakes and varying in taste depending on the brand, it can be added to casseroles, breads, and gravies or boldly sprinkled on salads and popcorn, mixed into dips, etc.

OILS we recommend are unrefined polyunsaturated sesame, corn, and safflower oil rather than name brand supermarket vegetable oils, usually overly processed and containing preservatives. Corn oil, with its buttery flavor, is a good choice for baking. Safflower oil, popular for its light taste, can easily become rancid; it is best to refrigerate all unrefined oils. Olive oil has some nutritional qualities that other oils do not and can be used in small quantities. Butter is a highly saturated fat and margarines are hydrogenated and highly processed. Use them in small quantities if at all; in most recipes, oils can be successfully substituted for either. Overall, we use as little butter or oil as possible in most recipes — just enough for good flavor.

Tofu and Tempeh Basics

Buying and Storing Tofu

There are different types of tofu to choose from. Soft tofu is best for "blended" recipes — dressings, dips, sauces, and puddings; it has more water content than firm and is less expensive. Firm or "pressed" tofu is best for main dishes, salads, and soups, where you want tofu to retain its shape. Tofu that is labeled neither soft nor firm can be used like soft tofu, where we call for "tofu" in our recipes or it can be pressed as follows: place ½ to ¾-inch slices of tofu on a plate or in a glass baking dish and cover the slices with a cutting board or another dish with a weight on top. Water will accumulate around the slices and can be poured off. Allow up to an hour for firmly pressed tofu.

Keep tofu refrigerated, stored in water in a closed container. If purchased water-packed and not to be used right away, drain and replace water. Change tofu water daily to ensure freshness up to a week or more. Tofu beginning to sour can be refreshed by simmering in boiling water for about 4 minutes.

Tofu can also be frozen; it takes on a porous texture (very chewy) and can be grated, shredded, or diced for use in sauces, as a ground beef replacement or a substitute for firm tofu. To freeze tofu, drain and place in a plastic bag, removing all air when you tie the bag shut. Thaw tofu in cool water or submerge in boiling water for 10 minutes, then rinse in cool water. Squeeze out excess water before using.

Buying and Storing Tempeh

Tempeh is sold in the frozen food section or dairy cooler of natural food stores and may be stored in the freezer until ready to use; some thawing will make cutting it a neater task. Dark spots on the cake are normal and do not indicate spoilage; there's no need to remove them. Tempeh should be cooked before eating.

Protein Complementarity

The protein value of both tofu and tempeh is increased as much as 40 percent when grains, bread, nuts, seeds, or dairy foods are eaten at the same meal.

Salads, Dressings, and Dips

Sunny Tofu Salad

1 lb firm or pressed tofu
2-4 tablespoons nutritional yeast (opt.)
1 tablespoon shoyu soy sauce or
   1-2 teaspoons light miso
1 clove garlic, crushed
¼ teaspoon turmeric
2 teaspoons prepared mustard
1 green onion, chopped
½ cup chopped celery
2-3 tablespoons lemon juice
mayonnaise or plain yogurt to taste (opt.)

Mash tofu with a fork or cut into small cubes. Add remaining ingredients, using enough lemon juice and mayonnaise or yogurt to give the taste and consistency you desire. Serve on a bed of greens, in a sandwich, or with crackers, or stuff a tomato with it and top with parsley.

Yield: about 2 cups

*TIPS ON MAKING DRESSINGS AND DIPS: All dressings and dips will stay fresher longer if you first steam the tofu 4-5 minutes and cool before blending. Tofu dressings can be served as dips or sauces for vegetables. The amount of water or other liquid is variable, depending on the firmness of tofu used and the consistency of dressing or dip desired.

"Nearly Chicken" Tempeh Salad

6 ounces tempeh
⅓ cup chopped celery or green pepper
¼ cup chopped parsley
1 green onion, chopped
⅓ cup tofu mayonnaise (page 8)
2 teaspoons prepared mustard
1 teaspoon shoyu soy sauce or ¼ teaspoon salt
¼ teaspoon turmeric
¼ teaspoon garlic powder
pinch of paprika

Cut tempeh into ⅓-inch cubes and steam in a vegetable steamer for 20 minutes; cool. Chop vegetables and put in large bowl. Mix mayonnaise with next 5 ingredients. Add tempeh to vegetables, stir in dressing, and chill.

Yield: 2 cups

VARIATIONS:

1) Add ½ teaspoon kelp for a **"Nearly Tuna" Salad.**
2) Add ⅓ cup chopped dill pickles and ½ teaspoon dill weed for a **Dilly Salad.**
3) Add ½ teaspoon cumin or 1 teaspoon curry powder for a **Curried Salad.**

Marinated Tofu Cubes for Salads

Make a marinade of equal parts shoyu soy sauce, lemon juice, and water. Add grated fresh ginger and/or crushed garlic to taste and a drop of Japanese sesame oil if desired. Marinate cubes of firm or pressed tofu several hours or several days. Add cubes to green salads, tabouli, pocket bread sandwiches....This is a great protein snack to keep on hand.

Cottage Tofu Spread

8 ounces firm or pressed tofu
2 or 3 umeboshi (pickled Japanese plums)
2 tablespoons chopped green onion tops
*   or 1 tablespoon chopped chives*
1-2 tablespoons chopped olives (opt.)

Mash tofu well with a fork or in a Japanese suribachi. Remove pits from the umeboshi. Add remaining ingredients to tofu and mix well; mixture should be light and fluffy. Refrigerate to let flavors blend. Umeboshi, available at natural food stores, provides the subtle tang in this delicious low-fat spread.

Yield: about 1 cup

Tofu Mayonnaise

1 lb tofu
¼ cup cider vinegar or lemon juice
  or a mixture of the two
½ teaspoon salt or 1 teaspoon light miso
½ teaspoon dry mustard or
  1 teaspoon prepared mustard
1 teaspoon honey (opt.)
¼ cup oil

Process ingredients in blender until very smooth, about 3 minutes. Less than one-third the calories of regular mayonnaise!

Yield: slightly more than 2 cups

Tofu Tartar Sauce

1 lb tofu
3 tablespoons oil
2-4 tablespoons lemon juice or rice vinegar
2 teaspoons honey
3 tablespoons chopped onion
¼ cup chopped parsley or celery leaves
½ teaspoon prepared mustard
¼ teaspoon salt or 1 teaspoon shoyu soy sauce
3 tablespoons chopped dill pickles

Process all but pickles in the blender until smooth, about three minutes. Add pickles and blend until fairly smooth. This dip is delicious with raw vegetables and crackers, on baked potatoes, or as a sandwich spread.

Yield: 2 cups

Tofu Sour Cream

1 lb tofu, sliced thick
1-2 tablespoons lemon juice
½ teaspoon salt or
  1 tablespoon shoyu soy sauce

Steam tofu 3-4 minutes unless it is very fresh; cool. Process ingredients in blender until smooth. Use as you would dairy sour cream, with one-third the calories!

Yield: 2 cups

Tofu Tahini Dressing

8 ounces tofu
½ cup water
¼ cup tahini
3 tablespoons lemon juice
2 teaspoons shoyu soy sauce
1 tablespoon oil
2 cloves garlic, crushed

Process all ingredients in blender until smooth. Add more lemon juice or water if needed; dressing will thicken when refrigerated.

Yield: about 1½ cups

Lemon Poppy Dressing

12 ounces tofu
¼ cup lemon juice
1 tablespoon cider vinegar (opt.)
1-2 teaspoons grated lemon peel
1 tablespoon poppy seeds
¼ cup chopped parsley
1 teaspoon shoyu soy sauce or
    1 teaspoon light miso

Process all ingredients in blender until smooth. Add up to 2 tablespoons water if needed.

Yield: about 2 cups

Tofu Russian Dressing

8 ounces tofu
2 teaspoons oil
2 tablespoons lemon juice
2 cloves garlic crushed
4 tablespoons natural ketchup
   or thick tomato sauce
1 teaspoon shoyu soy sauce
¼ teaspoon dill weed
½ teaspoon basil
½ teaspoon curry powder

Process all ingredients in blender until smooth.

Yield: about 1¼ cups

Tofu Mustard Dip

8 ounces tofu
1 tablespoon prepared mustard
¼ teaspoon turmeric
1-2 tablespoons lemon juice

Process all ingredients in blender until smooth. This makes a delicious sandwich/burger spread.

Yield: 1 cup

Garlic Dill Dip/Dressing

12 ounces tofu
1 tablespoon oil
2 teaspoons lemon juice or cider vinegar
1 teaspoon light miso or shoyu soy sauce
½ teaspoon dill weed
1 clove garlic, minced

For dip: Process all ingredients in blender.

For salad dressing: Blend as above, adding 1-2 teaspoons more lemon juice or vinegar and up to ¼ cup water as needed for dressing consistency.

Yield: 1½ cups

Deviled Tempeh Dip/Spread

6 ounces tempeh
2-3 tablespoons lemon juice
2-3 tablespoons safflower oil
½ cup water
2 tablespoons chopped onion
½ teaspoon prepared mustard
1 teaspoon shoyu soy sauce or
  ¼ teaspoon salt
¼ teaspoon turmeric
dash of cayenne
2 tablespoons chopped parsley

Dice tempeh and steam for 20 minutes; cool. Blend all ingredients except parsley until creamy. Stir in parsley. Chill to let flavors blend. The dip will thicken.

Yield: 1½ cups

Marinated Steamed Tempeh

Steam cubed tempeh as in **Deviled Tempeh Dip**, above. Then:
1) Marinate cubes with lightly steamed vegetables (broccoli, cauliflower, green beans, mushrooms, etc.) in your favorite vinaigrette dressing; or
2) Marinate cubes in equal parts shoyu soy sauce, lemon juice, and water, adding grated fresh ginger and/or crushed garlic to taste and a drop of Japanese sesame oil (opt.); add cubes to green or grain salads.

Tofu Cucumber Raita

12 ounces tofu
¼ cup lemon juice
½ teaspoon salt
1 teaspoon grated fresh ginger
1 large cucumber, peeled and chopped
1 green onion, chopped (opt.)

Process all ingredients in blender until smooth. (If desired, leave out ¼-½ cup cucumber, diced finely, and stir it into blended raita.) This is a good cooler to go with hot, spicy dishes like **Groundnut Stew** (page 44) or **Curried Tempeh or Tofu** (page 45). Refrigerate at least 2 hours to let flavors blend.

Yield: 2 cups

Creamy Curry Dip

8 ounces tofu
1-3 teaspoons curry powder
1-2 tablespoons lemon juice

Process all ingredients in blender until smooth. Serve with a fresh vegetable platter.

Yield: about 1 cup

Light Meals and Snacks

including appetizers and soups

Tofu Rice Burgers

1½ cups cooked brown rice
8 ounces tofu, drained and mashed
½ cup whole wheat flour
¼-½ cup chopped parsley
½ onion, chopped
½ cup raw or cooked vegetables,
 diced or grated (opt.)
1-2 cloves garlic, crushed
1 teaspoon cumin
1 teaspoon basil or thyme
1 tablespoon shoyu soy sauce
1 tablespoon tahini (opt.)
1-2 tablespoons water
wheat germ and sesame seeds

Combine all ingredients except wheat germ and sesame seeds. Include diced celery, zucchini, etc., if desired. Form patties and coat with wheat germ and seeds. Fry over medium heat or bake at 350° for 30 minutes. Serve on English muffins or whole wheat buns. Burgers are good cold, too; take a burger for lunch!

Yield: 5-6 burgers

Tempeh Burger or "TL&T"

Cook burger size pieces of tempeh in a covered, oiled skillet over medium high heat until browned, about 5 minutes per side. Add 1-2 tablespoons water and cover to steam cook 3-4 minutes. Serve in a sandwich with mayonnaise, lettuce, and tomato or other trimmings.

VARIATIONS:

1) Marinate tempeh in equal parts of lemon juice, shoyu soy sauce, and water before cooking.
2) Add crushed garlic, grated fresh ginger, or other herbs to marinade or to tempeh in skillet.
3) Serve as a main dish, covering the tempeh with mushroom gravy (page 40) and simmering for 6-8 minutes after "steam cooking" as above.

Down Home Corncakes

8 ounces tofu
1 egg, lightly beaten
2 cups whole kernel corn
  (cooked and cut from 2-3 ears of corn)
½ cup chopped green onions
¾ cup whole wheat flour
2-3 teaspoons shoyu soy sauce
½ small Jalapeno pepper, minced, or
  1 teaspoon Mexican hot sauce (opt.)
water as needed

Mash tofu well with a fork. Add remaining ingredients, in order, and mix well, adding up to ½ cup water if needed. Drop by heaping spoonfuls into hot, oiled skillet; fry until golden on both sides. Top with **Avocado Tofu Spread** (page 24) or **Tofu Sour Cream** (page 9).

Yield: about 20 small cakes

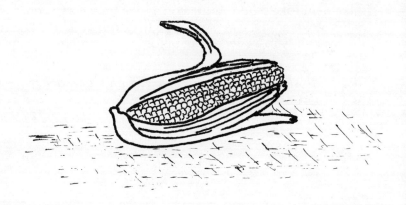

Thanks to Elisa Lottor, Santa Monica, California for this tasty recipe!

Spicy Tofu Paté

1 lb tofu
¼ cup whole wheat flour
¼ cup cornmeal
½ cup wheat germ
¼ cup corn oil
2 tablespoons shoyu soy sauce
1 teaspoon molasses (opt.)
½ teaspoon ground fennel
2 teaspoons garlic powder
¼ teaspoon savory
¼ teaspoon celery seed
1 teaspoon powdered sage
½ teaspoon allspice
2 teaspoons oregano
2-3 teaspoons prepared mustard

Mash tofu in a large bowl. Add remaining ingredients and mix well with hands. Pack into oiled cans or a small oiled casserole dish and cover with 2-3 paper towels or aluminum foil; steam for 25-35 minutes on a rack inside a covered pot on the stove or in a pan of water in the oven at 375°. The top will be slightly browned. Cool before removing from cans or dish.

The steaming blends the flavors. The paté can be stored in the refrigerator for up to two weeks.

Yield: about 2½ cups

VARIATIONS/USES:

1) **Soy Paté** — Serve "as is" (cold) with crackers or dark bread.
2) **Spicy Soy Patties** — Add 1 tablespoon corn oil per cup of paté; knead in. Form into patties and fry over medium heat until lightly browned. Serve on whole wheat bread for lunch or with scrambled tofu for a hot breakfast or Sunday brunch.
3) **No-Meat Balls** — Add corn oil as above, or 1 egg for every 2 cups of paté mixture, and form into bite-size balls. Place on oiled cookie sheet, and bake at 375° for 25-30 minutes, until browned. Cover with a spicy tomato sauce and serve as an hors d'oeuvre or serve with your favorite spaghetti sauce over pasta.
4) **Pizza Topping** — Crumble paté mixture onto your favorite pizza for a new treat.

Tofu Jerky

Slice 1 lb firm or pressed tofu into 3/8-inch slices or strips. Marinate in the following mixture for at least 2 hours, turning at least once:
¼ cup shoyu soy sauce
¼ cup water or broth
3 tablespoons lemon juice
½ teaspoon garlic powder
1 teaspoon molasses
2 teaspoons prepared mustard

Drain and place directly on an oiled rack in a 375° oven. Bake 40-50 minutes until firm and dry, turning once.

Jerky strips are great for quick snacks, on a relish tray with **Tofu Mustard Dip**, or for backpacking. They will keep well, refrigerated, for 3-4 weeks, so make up a bunch at one time.

Tofu Jerky II

Subsitute 3 tablespoons Dr. Bronner's Mineral Broth and ½ cup water for the shoyu and water above. Leave out the molasses. Try both recipes!

Stir-Fried Tofu

1 medium onion, chopped
1 large clove garlic, minced
1 tablespoon oil
1 lb firm or pressed tofu
¼ teaspoon turmeric
2-3 teaspoons shoyu soy sauce
1 teaspoon dill weed
½ teaspoon cumin
pinch of salt
1-2 tablespoons nutritional yeast flakes (opt.)

Sauté onion and garlic in hot, oiled wok or skillet. Add tofu, cut into 1-inch cubes. Cook 2 minutes, stirring gently. Add turmeric and shoyu. Keep turning tofu to brown on all sides. Add dill, cumin and salt. When nearly browned, add yeast and cook 1 minute more. Serve with brown rice or in pocket bread with sprouts.

Serves 4

VARIATION: Sauté vegetables such as green pepper, zucchini, mushrooms, tomatoes, or bean sprouts before adding tofu, remove from wok or skillet, then return as tofu finishes cooking.

Scrambled Tofu

8 ounces firm or pressed tofu
¼ teaspoon turmeric
½ teaspoon prepared mustard
1 tablespoon chopped parsley
 or ¼ teaspoon dill weed
pinch of salt
2 teaspoons oil
optional: diced green onion, mushrooms, green pepper

With a fork, scramble tofu in a bowl with turmeric, mustard, parsley, and salt. Heat oil in a small skillet; cook tofu for 4-5 minutes, stirring gently. If using vegetables, sauté them one minute, then cook with tofu. For an egg consistency, scramble an egg with the tofu before sautéing. Serve with whole wheat toast or English muffins.

Serves 2

Deep-Fried Tempeh

This is a traditional Indonesian method of cooking tempeh. Fried at the proper temperature, tempeh will absorb a minimum of oil and not taste greasy.

Pour oil in a wok or skillet to fill 1½ to 2 inches and heat to 350°. An electric skillet with temperature guage is good for this. Gently drop in ¼-inch slices or strips of tempeh. Maintain temperature so that tempeh strips sink briefly, then rise to the surface. Simmer 3-4 minutes, until golden brown. Drain on absorbent paper. Use in sandwiches, as an hors d'oeuvre with dips, etc.

VARIATIONS:

1) Briefly marinate tempeh in ½ cup water (or ¼ cup water and ¼ cup lemon juice), 1 teaspoon salt or shoyu soy sauce and your choice of seasonings: grated fresh ginger, crushed garlic, ½ teaspoon coriander or curry powder. Drain tempeh pieces on absorbent paper and then proceed to deep-fry.
2) For a crispier tempeh, dust marinated tempeh pieces with whole wheat or brown rice flour before frying.

Shallow-Fried Tempeh

This is a basic method of cooking tempeh. Fry ½-inch strips or cubes to give salads additional protein and flavor or serve with dips as appetizers.

Cut tempeh into strips or cubes and fry in oil in a wok or skillet until crisp and brown. A skillet will need about ¼ inch oil. Drain well on absorbent paper. For a richer flavor, marinate tempeh as in recipe for **Deep-Fried Tempeh.**

Avocado Tofu Spread

Mash 1 ripe avocado with about 8 ounces drained, mashed tofu — about half and half — and add 1 tablespoon lemon juice, 1-2 tablespoons chopped onion, 1-2 teaspoons shoyu soy sauce, and a dash of hot sauce, if desired. This is a great way to stretch an avocado and enjoy a rather high fat food with fewer calories.

Peanutty Tofu Spread

This is a delicious spread, better than either tofu or peanut butter alone.

Mix ½ cup peanut butter with 8 ounces mashed tofu, adding if desired: 1) 1 mashed banana, 1 tablespoon lemon juice, and 1-2 teaspoons honey, 2) 1-2 tablespoons lemon juice and 1 teaspoon miso, or 3) ¼ cup chopped dates and 2-4 tablespoons ground toasted sunflower seeds.

Also great for sandwiches and crackers are: **Cottage Tofu Spread** *(page 7) and* **Deviled Tempeh Spread** *(page 13).*

Soups

Soy for Soups! Soups for Soy!

Add pressed, cubed tofu or cubed tempeh, uncooked or shallow-fried, to your favorite soups for a protein boost. Try tofu in cold, spicy gazpacho, miso-onion soup, or lentil stew. Add uncooked or fried tempeh to minestrone and other thick soups...and don't forget it when making spaghetti sauce!

Miso-Tofu Soup

1 small onion, chopped
1 carrot, sliced
1 stalk celery, sliced
1 cup chopped vegetables
   (green pepper, mushrooms, zucchini, etc.)
2 cups water or vegetable stock
6 ounces firm or pressed tofu, cubed
1 cup chopped spinach or other greens
2 tablespoons miso
1 tablespoon tahini (opt.)

Put vegetables in saucepan with water or stock and bring to a simmer. Cook until vegetables are tender, about 8-10 minutes. Add tofu cubes and greens. Remove ¼ cup of soup broth and combine it with miso and tahini to make a paste. Stir paste into soup, remove from heat, and serve. Easy and quick!

Serves 2-3

NOTE: For a heartier soup add leftover cooked brown rice, barley, millet, or Japanese buckwheat noodles. Why not try miso soup for breakfast like the Japanese do.

Fruity Crepes

Delectable for breakfast, brunch, or dessert.

1 egg
2 cups water
1¾ cups whole wheat pastry flour
¼ teaspoon salt

Place all ingredients, in order, in blender and process at low speed for 2-3 minutes. Let mixture sit for 15 minutes. Brush an 8-inch crepe pan or small skillet with corn oil; when hot, pour a scant 1/4 cup of batter into center of pan and quickly tilt pan in all directions so batter spreads evenly. Cook 3 minutes on first side, flip, and cook 1 minute longer. Cool on a rack. Continue with remaining batter — a second pan quickens the process. Fill each crepe with 3-4 tablespoons of filling, roll up, and place in an oiled baking dish. Cover with sauce and bake at 350° for 20 minutes.

Yield: 12 crepes

APPLE TOFU FILLING

8 ounces tofu
1 tablespoon honey
¼ teaspoon vanilla
2 teaspoons lemon juice
1 teaspoon cinnamon
1 tablespoon whole wheat flour
3 cups diced apples
½ cup chopped dates
½ cup water
¼ cup roasted sunflower seeds

Process first six ingredients in blender until smooth. Cook apples and dates in water over medium heat for 6-7 minutes; cool. Combine both mixtures and seeds in a bowl. Let sit 30 minutes for flavors to blend. *Fills 12 crepes.*

BLUEBERRY TOFU FILLING

10 ounces tofu
2 tablespoons honey
¼ teaspoon vanilla
2 teaspoons lemon juice
½ teaspoon grated lemon peel
2¼ cups blueberries
½ cup chopped walnuts

In a medium-size bowl mash tofu with honey, vanilla, lemon juice, and lemon peel. Stir in blueberries and walnuts and let sit 30 minutes. *Fills 12 crepes.*

ORANGE SAUCE

1 cup orange juice
1-2 tablespoons honey
1 tablespoon arrowroot or cornstarch
2 tablespoons cold water

Heat orange juice and honey in a small saucepan. Dissolve arrowroot in cold water and add to orange juice, stirring over medium heat until thick, about 3-4 minutes.

VARIATION: For an *Apple "Sauce"* substitute 1 cup apple juice for the orange juice and add ½ teaspoon grated lemon or orange peel.

Spinach Crepes

Make crepes as above. Fill with **Creamed Spinach** (page 41). Sprinkle toasted sesame meal on top; bake at 350° for 25 minutes. Serve with **Tofu Mustard Dip** (page 12).

Serves 6

Walnut Balls With
Tofu Lemon Cream Sauce

2 cups finely chopped walnuts
½ cup wheat germ
3 tablespoons chopped parsley
¼ cup chopped green onion
6 ounces tofu
5 tablespoons water
2 teaspoons lemon juice
¼ cup whole wheat flour
1 clove garlic, crushed
1 teaspoon prepared mustard
pinch of salt

Combine 1¼ cups walnuts, wheat germ, onion, and parsley in a bowl. Process remaining ingredients in blender until smooth and combine with nut mixture. Form walnut size balls, rolling each in reserved nuts. Place on oiled baking sheet. Bake at 350° for 35-40 minutes. Serve hot with Tofu Lemon Cream Sauce. Makes 20 delicious bite-size balls. A great appetizer!

TOFU LEMON CREAM SAUCE: Process 6 ounces tofu and 5 tablespoons lemon juice in blender until smooth. Heat ¾ cup water in a small saucepan. Dissolve 1 tablespoon arrowroot or cornstarch in 2 tablespoons cold water and add to saucepan, stirring until thickened. When thickened, add blender mixture and 2 tablespoons chopped parsley. Add salt to taste. When hot, pour over baked Walnut Balls and serve.

Main Courses

entrees to please all

Tempeh Shish Kebabs

This is a delicious and nearly oil-free way of serving tempeh, great for summer parties. An outdoor grill is not necessary; an oven broiler will work.

8 ounces tempeh
2-3 tablespoons shoyu soy sauce
3 tablespoons dry white wine
3 tablespoons water or stock
1 tablespoon lemon juice
1-1½ teaspoons Japanese sesame oil
½ teaspoon grated fresh ginger
1-2 cloves garlic, crushed
¼ teaspoon dry mustard
1 teaspoon honey (opt.)
vegetables

Cut tempeh into 1-inch cubes. Steam 20 minutes; cool. Combine remaining ingredients and marinate tempeh in sauce for at least 30 minutes on each side.

To assemble KEBABS: alternate tempeh with slices of mushroom, green pepper, onion, zucchini, and tomatoes on stainless steel skewers or bamboo skewers which have been soaked in salt water. Grill, basting with marinade, until nicely browned. Serve with brown rice or bulgur.

Serves 3-4

Tofu Moussaka

2 medium eggplants
olive oil
1 large onion, diced
1 green pepper, diced
1½ cups sliced mushrooms
2 cloves garlic, minced
1 quart tomato sauce
1 bay leaf
1 teaspoon oregano
2 teaspoons basil
3 tablespoons chopped parsley
1 teaspoon cinnamon
⅓ cup red wine (opt.)
2 cups tofu cream sauce (below)
¼ cup grated Parmesan cheese (opt.)
¼ teaspoon nutmeg

TOFU CREAM SAUCE:

1 lb tofu, lightly pressed
1 tablespoon lemon juice
1-2 teaspoons olive oil
1 tablespoon whole wheat flour
2 tablespoons chopped parsley
pinch of salt
1 egg, beaten (opt.)
½ cup grated Parmesan cheese (opt.)

Peel and slice eggplant into ⅓-inch slices and brush lightly with olive oil; broil until lightly browned. In a large skillet, sauté onion, green pepper, mushrooms, and garlic until onion is clear. Add remaining ingredients, except tofu cream sauce, cheese, and nutmeg. Let the tomato sauce simmer for 30-60 minutes.

Make TOFU CREAM SAUCE by mashing tofu with lemon juice, oil, whole wheat flour, parsley, and salt. Stir in egg and cheese.

To assemble: Layer eggplant in an oiled 9 × 13 baking dish. Cover with tomato sauce and spoon Tofu Cream Sauce on top. Sprinkle additional ¼ cup cheese and nutmeg on top and bake at 350° for 35 minutes. This is better the second day and even better the third!

Serves 6-8

VARIATION: Add 6-8 ounces of ground tempeh to the tomato sauce for a thicker, more substantial dish.

Lasagna

Not as heavy as meat/cheese lasagna, yet a filling and delicious crowd pleaser.

10-12 ounces lasagna noodles
½ teaspoon salt
10-12 ounces tempeh, cut into ¼-inch cubes
2 tablespoons olive oil
1 medium onion, diced
1 medium green pepper, diced
1 cup diced mushrooms
1-2 cloves garlic, minced
3 tablespoons chopped parsley
1 tablespoon oregano
2-3 teaspoons basil
3-4 cups tomato sauce
1 large bunch spinach
24 ounces tofu, drained
½ teaspoon salt
½-1 cup grated mozzarella cheese (opt.)
1 large tomato, sliced

Cook noodles in boiling salted water until done, about 12-15 minutes; drain. In a large skillet sauté tempeh, onion, pepper, mushrooms, and garlic in olive oil for 5-7 minutes, stirring occasionally. Add parsley, oregano, basil, and tomato sauce; simmer for 30-60 minutes. Meanwhile, wash, drain, and chop spinach and steam lightly, 2 to 3 minutes. Mash tofu, adding salt and spinach.

Assemble in an oiled 9 × 13 baking dish as follows: noodles, ½ of the tofu mixture, ⅓ of the tomato sauce, noodles, ½ tofu mixture, ⅓ tomato sauce, noodles, remaining sauce, cheese and tomato slices. Bake at 350° for 20-25 minutes.

Serves 6-8

NOTE: Tempeh may be omitted and more vegetables added — try diced, steamed zucchini or eggplant. For a spicy flavor, add ¼ teaspoon cayenne to tomato sauce.

Barbecued Tempeh

"Barbecued ribs" — vegetarian style — a real company pleaser.

20 ounces tempeh
3 tablespoons olive oil
1 large onion, chopped
1-2 cloves garlic, minced
12 ounces tomato paste
3 cups water or stock
2-3 tablespoons cider vinegar
2-3 tablespoons molasses
1 tablespoon shoyu soy sauce
½ teaspoon dry mustard
½-1 teaspoon grated fresh ginger
pinch of cayenne (opt.)

Cut tempéh into strips 2-2½ inches long. Sauté in 2 tablespoons oil in wok or skillet until browned on all sides; set aside. Sauté onion, green pepper, and garlic in 1 tablespoon oil. Add remaining ingredients and simmer 10-15 minutes. Add tempeh strips and simmer 5-10 minutes more, or longer for a full barbecue flavor. Serve with tossed salad, brown rice, and garlic bread.

Serves 4-5

Tempeh "Sloppy Joes"

For kids of all ages — a tasty surprise!

20 ounces tempeh, crumbled
2 tablespoons oil
Sauce as for Barbecued Tempeh,
  without the ginger
2-3 teaspoons chili powder
Additional water as needed

Sauté crumbled tempeh in oil until well browned. Prepare sauce as above, adding chili powder. Add tempeh and simmer 10-15 minutes. Serve over whole wheat English muffins or buns.

Serves 5-6

Tempeh or Tofu Burritos

3 tablespoons oil
20 ounces tempeh, ground or crumbled
1 large onion, diced
1 cup diced mushrooms
2½ teaspoons chili powder
1½ teaspoons cumin
1½ teaspoons coriander
½ teaspoon basil
1 teaspoon chopped parsley
¼ cup nutritional yeast (opt.)
2 tablespoons shoyu soy sauce
2 cups tomato sauce
6 chapaties or whole wheat tortillas

Heat oil in a large skillet; sauté tempeh, onions, and mushrooms about 10 minutes. Add spices and herbs and cook 10-15 minutes more. Stir in yeast and shoyu; remove from heat. Prepare your favorite tomato sauce and mix 1 cup sauce with tempeh mixture. Fill 6 chapaties or tortillas and place in oiled baking dish. Top with remaining tomato sauce and bake 20 minutes at 350°. Serve with hot sauce, yogurt, and sprouts.

Serves 4-6

VARIATION:
Use 24 ounces firm or pressed tofu instead of tempeh. Crumble and prepare as above, reducing skillet cooking time.

Credit to Zoo's Zoo's Restaurant Collective, Eugene, Oregon, for this delectable dish.

Tempeh or Tofu with Sesame Miso Sauce

2-3 tablespoons oil
10 ounces tempeh or 12 ounces firm or
  pressed tofu, cut into ¾-inch cubes
2 cups chopped vegetables
  (onion, green pepper, zucchini, etc.)
2 tablespoons tahini
2 tablespoons miso
1 teaspoon grated fresh ginger
¾ cup water or stock

Heat oil in wok or skillet. Sauté tempeh (steamed first in a vegetable steamer for 15 minutes) or tofu with the vegetables over medium heat. When tempeh or tofu is browned and vegetables are crisp-tender, remove to a bowl. Mix the remaining ingredients and cook 1-2 minutes over medium heat. Stir in vegetable mixture and cook 1-2 minutes, until hot. Serve with brown rice.

Serves 3

Savory Tofu Pie

FILLING:

24 ounces firm or pressed tofu
3 tablespoons oil
1 teaspoon lemon juice
1-2 tablespoons water
¼ teaspoon salt
onion essence (below)
¼ cup sliced ripe olives, and/or
   1-2 cups sliced, sauteed mushrooms
1 cup chopped spinach or chard (opt.)
2 tablespoons finely chopped parsley

ONION ESSENCE:

1 cup diced onion
2-3 cloves garlic, minced
3-4 tablespoons shoyu soy sauce
½ teaspoon molasses
1 teaspoon thyme leaves (opt.)
1 teaspoon oil

Simmer together in a small skillet, covered, until onions are soft, about 15 minutes.

Preheat oven to 350°. Grate tofu. Put half in the blender with oil, lemon juice, and salt, and blend until smooth; add water as needed. In a mixing bowl, combine remaining grated tofu, onion essence, olives and/or mushrooms, and steamed, drained spinach or other vegetables, if desired. Stir in half of blender mixture. Spoon into partially baked **Mixed Grain Crust** and spread the remainder of the blended tofu-oil mixture over all. Sprinkle with parsley. Bake 25 to 30 minutes. Allow to stand 10 minutes before cutting to serve.

Serves 6-8

MIXED GRAIN CRUST:

½ cup millet, ground to a fine meal in blender
¼ cup cornmeal
½ cup whole wheat pastry flour
pinch salt
2 tablespoons oil
4-6 tablespoons water

Briefly toast millet meal and cornmeal in a dry skillet until it just begins to smell fragrant. Immediately pour into a mixing bowl and mix in pastry flour and salt. Stir in oil briskly with a fork. Add water and mix well. Mixture should be moist but not gooey. Press into oiled 9-inch pie dish with fingers. Bake 5 minutes at 350°, add filling, and bake as instructed.

This delicious recipe is adapted with permission from **Laurel's Kitchen 1980 Calendar**, © 1979 by Nilgiri Press, Petaluma, CA.

Baked Marinated Tofu

1 lb firm or pressed tofu
2 tablespoons shoyu soy sauce
⅓ cup water
1-2 teaspoons lemon juice
½ teaspoon grated fresh ginger

Cut tofu into ½-inch slices. Mix the remaining ingredients and pour over the slices in a shallow baking dish. Marinate 30 minutes, turning once. Cover dish and bake for 30 minutes at 350°. Turn once and remove cover for last 10 minutes.

Serve as hot **Tofu Cutlets**, garnished with mushroom gravy (below) and/or chopped green onions, or cool and use as **Everyday Tofu**, cubed or in thin slices, for salads and sandwiches. Add cubes to stir-fried vegetable dishes. Serve cubes on toothpicks as an hors d'oeuvre. Easy and versatile!

MUSHROOM GRAVY: Steam ¼ lb mushrooms, sliced, and ¼ cup diced onion for 4-5 minutes, using 1½ cups water; reserve the stock. Grind ½ cup cashews to a fine powder in a blender; add ½ cup of the stock and blend. In a small saucepan, combine this cream with the remainder of the stock, the vegetables, and 1 tablespoon shoyu soy sauce; simmer for 3-4 minutes. Dissolve 1 tablespoon arrowroot or cornstarch in 2 tablespoons cold water and add to saucepan, stirring for 3-5 minutes until it thickens. Add 1 teaspoon grated fresh ginger, if desired.

Yield: about 1½ cups

Creamed Spinach

2 large bunches spinach
2 tablespoons water
8 ounces tofu
2 cloves garlic, minced
1 teaspoon shoyu soy sauce
1 teaspoon lemon juice
½ teaspoon dill weed or oregano
½ teaspoon dry mustard
1 teaspoon butter or oil
ground toasted sesame seeds or gomashio

Wash and chop spinach and put in saucepan with water. Simmer until cooked, about 5 minutes. Drain, reserving cooking water. Prepare sauce: Put tofu in blender with ½ cup cooking water and next 5 ingredients; blend until smooth. Pour sauce onto spinach in pot, add butter or oil, and reheat over low heat until hot. Serve as a side dish or over rice or whole wheat English muffins for a main course. Garnish with sesame seeds or gomasio.

Serves 3

Spinach Noodle Casserole

Prepare creamed spinach as above, using 1 bunch spinach and doubling the sauce. Add ¼-½ teaspoon nutmeg. Cook 6 ounces whole wheat noodles. Combine noodles, cooked spinach sauce, 2 chopped green onions, and ¼ lb sauteed mushrooms (opt.). Turn into oiled casserole dish and top with ¼ cup toasted ground sesame seeds or gomashio. Bake at 350° for about 30 minutes.

Serves 4

Hearty Stew with Corn Dumplings

2 medium onions, chopped
3 tablespoons olive oil
5-6 cloves garlic, minced
1 teaspoon ground cumin
½ teaspoon ground cinnamon
½ cup diced hot green chilis, canned,
   or 1 fresh hot pepper, minced
6 cups tomatoes with liquid
1 lb yellow squash, summer or winter, sliced
1½ teaspoons salt
1½ cups water
8 ounces tempeh, cubed
1 lb zucchini, sliced
8 ounces pressed tofu, cubed
3-4 tablespoons fresh cilantro or
   1 tablespoon ground coriander
1 teaspoon honey (opt.)

Sauté onions in oil in a large pot. When clear, add garlic, cumin, cinnamon, and chilis. Sauté several minutes more. Add tomatoes and liquid, winter squash (if using summer squash, add later, with zucchini), salt, water, and tempeh. Lower heat, cover pot, and simmer 45 minutes. (Meanwhile, prepare dumpling batter.) Add zucchini, summer squash, tofu, cilantro, and honey. Cook 5 minutes more. Drop dumpling batter in stew by spoonfuls. Cover pot and simmer 20 minutes.

Serves 6

DUMPLINGS:

1 cup cornmeal
⅓ cup whole wheat flour
1 teaspoon baking powder
½ teaspoon salt
½ cup milk (soy or dairy)
½ teaspoon honey
1 tablespoon corn oil
1 egg

Sift together dry ingredients. Beat together milk, honey, oil, and egg; add to dry ingredients and stir just until batter is smooth.

Groundnut Stew

Peanuts are "groundnuts" in Africa. This West African spicy stew is an adaptation of the traditional recipe.

1 large onion, chopped
1 large green pepper, chopped
2 cloves garlic, minced
1 tablespoon oil
1 lb firm or pressed tofu, cubed
  (or frozen, thawed tofu, cubed)
2 large fresh tomatoes, skinned and chopped
2 tablespoons chopped parsley
18 ounces tomato paste
3 cups vegetable stock
½ cup peanut butter
salt or shoyu soy sauce to taste
¼-½ teaspoon cayenne
2 teaspoons basil

In a large soup kettle, sauté onions, pepper, and garlic in oil until onions are clear. Stir in tofu, tomatoes, and parsley. Process the remaining ingredients in a blender and add to the pot. Simmer for 1-2 hours for fullest flavor. Serve over steamed brown rice with **Tofu Cucumber Raita** (page 14) on the side.

Serves 6-8

VARIATION: For **Groundnut Soup**, add 1-2 cups additional chopped vegetables (zucchini, eggplant, cauliflower, etc.) and 1-2 more cups of vegetable stock during the last 30 minutes of cooking. Serve with whole wheat bread and a dish of **Tofu Cucumber Raita** (page 14) on the side.

Curried Tempeh

2 tablespoons oil
1 medium onion, chopped
1 clove garlic, minced
½-1 teaspoon grated fresh ginger
8 ounces tempeh, cut into ½-inch cubes
5 whole cloves
¼ teaspoon cinnamon
1 inch hot dried pepper, minced, or
    ½ teaspoon cayenne
1 parsnip, sliced
1 teaspoon cumin
½ teaspoon turmeric
1 teaspoon coriander
½ teaspoon salt
½ cup water or vegetable stock
¼ cup raw cashews or peanuts
2 cups broccoli or cauliflower pieces
2 teaspoons arrowroot or cornstarch
2 tablespoons cold water
shoyu soy sauce to taste

Heat 1 tablespoon oil in wok or skillet; sauté onion, garlic, and ginger until onion is clear. Add cloves, cinnamon, and hot pepper. Stir and add 1 tablespoon oil and tempeh cubes. Cook, stirring, and after 5 minutes add parsnip. Continue cooking on medium heat. Add remaining spices and salt and cook 1-2 minutes more. Add stock, nuts, and broccoli. Simmer, covered, for 10 minutes. Dissolve arrowroot in cold water and stir in until sauce thickens. Add shoyu to taste. Serve with brown rice and **Tofu Cucumber Raita** (page 14).

Serves 3-4

For **Curried Tofu**, substitute 12 ounces firm or pressed tofu, cubed, for the tempeh; add with the nuts and broccoli. Continue recipe as above.

45

Desserts

nutritious delicacies to satisfy the sweet tooth

yummy

Tofu Cheesecake

FILLING:

20 ounces firmly pressed tofu
¼ cup lemon juice
5-6 tablespoons honey
1 teaspoon vanilla
1 teaspoon grated lemon peel
2 tablespoons whole wheat flour
2 tablespoons butter or safflower oil

FRUIT TOPPING (opt.):

1¼ cups blueberries, cherries, sliced peaches,
    or strawberries
4-6 tablespoons water, depending on fruit used
2-4 tablespoons honey
1 tablespoon arrowroot or cornstarch
2 tablespoons cold water
1 teaspoon lemon juice

Preheat oven to 350°. Process all filling ingredients in blender until smooth. Pour into 9-inch **Crumb Crust** (page 52) and bake for 40-45 minutes. Meanwhile, make Fruit Topping: Cook fruit with water and honey over low heat for 5 minutes. Dissolve arrowroot in cold water and lemon juice and stir into cooked fruit. Cook 2 minutes more, stirring until thickened. Spoon onto top of pie for the last 5 minutes of baking time. Chill several hours before serving.

Serves 8-12

Pumpkin Pie

This is a delicious, light pumpkin pie!

FILLING:

8 ounces tofu
2 cups pureed pumpkin or winter squash
6 tablespoons honey
2 tablespoons molasses
½ teaspoon powdered ginger
1 teaspoon cinnamon
¼ teaspoon cloves or nutmeg
1 tablespoon whole wheat flour

Preheat oven to 350°. Process all ingredients in a blender until very smooth. Pour into partially baked **Rice Crust** (page 52) and bake for 35-40 minutes. Chill for 2 hours before serving. Serve topped with **Tofu Creme** (page 49).

Serves 8

Tofu Creme

The versatile sweet creme — use as a dessert topping, a filling for cream puffs, a frosting, or combine with fresh fruit for a summer parfait.

1 lb firm or pressed tofu
2-4 tablespoons cashews
½ cup water
4-6 tablespoons honey or maple syrup
1½ teaspoons vanilla
pinch salt
¼ teaspoon cinnamon (opt.)

Steam tofu 3-4 minutes; cool. Whirl nuts in the blender until they become a fine powder; add water to make a cashew milk. Reserve half of this milk. Add remaining ingredients to the blender and process until very smooth, adding more of the cashew milk if necessary.

Yield: 2½ cups

VARIATION: For a mocha mousse or frosting, add 1 tablespoon carob powder or 1 tablespoon coffee substitute powder or 1½ teaspoons of each.

Peach Tofu Pie

¼ lb dried peaches
½ teaspoon cinnamon
1 tablespoon arrowroot or cornstarch
2 tablespoons cold water
12 ounces tofu, drained
2 tablespoons butter or oil
2 tablespoons lemon juice
1 teaspoon grated lemon peel
6 tablespoons honey
1 teaspoon vanilla (opt.)

Preheat oven to 350°. Simmer dried peaches and cinnamon in water to cover until tender, about 10 minutes. Drain and set aside fruit, reserving cooking liquid. Dissolve arrowroot in cold water and add to ½ cup reserved liquid, stirring over medium heat until thickened. Pour in blender with remaining ingredients, except the peaches. Blend until smooth, adding more fruit liquid or lemon juice if needed. Pour into 8-inch **Crumb Crust** (page 52) and decorate with chopped peaches. Bake for 30 minutes. Chill several hours before serving.

Serves 6-8

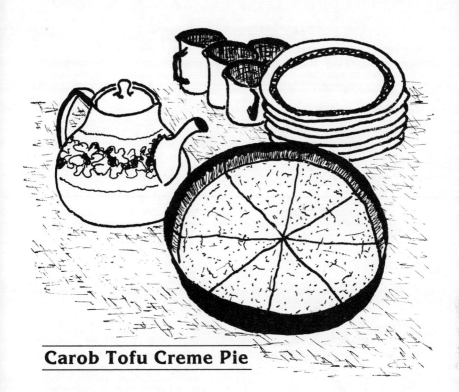

Carob Tofu Creme Pie

1 lb tofu
6-8 tablespoons honey
2-4 tablespoons milk or water
2 tablespoons peanut butter
4 tablespoons light carob powder, sifted
1 teaspoon vanilla

Preheat oven to 325°. Process filling ingredients in blender until smooth, using as much milk or water as is needed. Pour into 9-inch **Crumb Crust** or **Rice Crust** (page 52) and bake for 45 minutes. Serve chilled.

Serves 8

VARIATION: For a **Mocha Tofu Pie**, use 1 tablespoon less carob and add 1½ tablespoons coffee substitute and ½ teaspoon allspice.

Pastry Crusts

Rice Flour Crust

1 cup brown rice flour
½ cup whole wheat pastry flour
¼ cup finely ground nutmeats (opt.)
¼ teaspoon salt
¼ cup butter or 3 tablespoons oil and
  1 tablespoon Tofu Creme (page 49)
5-6 tablespoons cold water

Combine flour, nutmeats, and salt in a medium-size mixing bowl. Cut butter or oil and Tofu Creme into the flour with a pastry cutter or a fork. Add water and blend in with pastry cutter or fork until you can form a ball of dough with your hands. Chill the dough for 20 minutes and then roll out between sheets of waxed paper. Gently place in a 9-inch pie pan and form crust edge with your fingers. Bake at 350° for 5 minutes before adding filling.

Crumb Crust

1¼ cups granola
½ cup whole wheat flour
3 tablespoons melted butter or oil

Whirl granola in blender for 30 seconds. Combine with remaining ingredients. Pat into an 8- or 9-inch pie pan. Chill while preparing filling.

Tofu Rice Pudding

2 cups cooked short-grain brown rice
8 ounces tofu or frozen tofu, crumbled
½ cup raisins, simmered in ½ cup water until soft
3-5 tablespoons honey or maple syrup
1 crisp apple, sliced thin or chopped
½ teaspoon cinnamon
1 teaspoon vanilla
pinch of cardamom

Preheat oven to 350°. Combine all ingredients in a mixing bowl, adding more water if necessary. Bake in an oiled baking dish for 35-40 minutes. Serve as is or topped with **Tofu Creme** (page 49).

Serves 4

VARIATION: For a creamier pudding, blend the tofu (not frozen) with sweetener and juice from cooked raisins.

Tofu Banana Pudding

8 ounces tofu
2 small bananas, mashed
1 tablespoon lemon juice
1-2 tablespoons honey
1 teaspoon vanilla
1 tablespoon tahini (opt.)

Process ingredients in blender until smooth. Add milk or fruit juice if more liquid is needed. Chill 30 minutes.

Serves 2-3

VARIATIONS: Add a few chopped dates or raisins; substitute a fresh, sliced peach or ¾ cup strawberries or blackberries for one of the bananas; or add 1 tablespoon peanut butter instead of tahini. Garnish with fresh fruit or chopped nuts.

Tofu Peanut Cookies

½ cup butter
1 cup peanut butter
8 ounces tofu
6-8 tablespoons honey
2 tablespoons molasses
½ teaspoon baking powder
½ cup wheat germ
1 cup whole wheat pastry flour
4 tablespoons carob chips (opt.)
2-3 tablespoons sunflower seeds (opt.)

Preheat oven to 375°. Cream butter and peanut butter. Blend tofu, honey, and molasses in blender and mix with creamed butters. Combine dry ingredients and add to wet. Drop by spoonfuls onto oiled cookie sheet. Press surface with a fork. Bake 10-12 minutes or until lightly browned.

Makes 4 dozen small cookies

Tofu-Herb Muffins

2 tablespoons minced onion
1 tablespoon corn oil
10 ounces tofu, mashed well
1 tablespoon honey
½ teaspoon salt
1 tablespoon active dry yeast
¼ cup warm water
1 beaten egg or 2 more ounces tofu,
   mashed well
2½ cups whole wheat flour
1½ teaspoons dill weed
½ teaspoon each basil and thyme

Saute onion in oil until soft. Add tofu, honey, and salt and heat mixture to lukewarm. In a medium-size bowl, dissolve yeast in warm water, adding a drop of honey and ¼ cup of the flour. Let this mixture sit for 15 minutes until it becomes bubbly. Stir in egg (or 2 more ounces tofu), herbs, 1 cup of the flour, and the onion-tofu mixture. Mix well and add remaining flour, mixing thoroughly. Turn onto a floured surface and knead for 5 minutes. Place in a greased bowl, cover, and let rise for 1-1½ hours or until doubled in bulk. Punch dough down and divide into 12 balls, kneading and forming each ball. Place in greased muffin tins. Let rise 30-40 minutes. Preheat oven to 400°. Bake 15 minutes.

Yield: 1 dozen muffins

Creme Puffs à la Tofu

¾ cup water
⅓ cup corn oil or butter
pinch of salt
¾ cup whole wheat pastry flour
3 large eggs

Preheat oven to 400°. In a medium-size saucepan bring water, oil, and salt to a boil. Remove from heat and quickly add flour. Return saucepan to burner and over low heat beat mixture continuously with a wooden spoon until it forms a ball and leaves sides of pan. Remove from heat. With an electric mixer or wooden spoon beat in eggs, one at a time, beating until the dough is shiny and breaks away in strands. It will be stiff. Drop by rounded tablespoons, 2 inches apart, on an ungreased cookie sheet. Shape into 8 puffs. Bake for 35-40 minutes or until puffed and golden. Cool on rack. Fill with **Tofu Creme** (page 49) and top with Carob Sauce.

Yield: 8 creme puffs

CAROB SAUCE:

1 tablespoon butter
¼ cup honey or maple syrup
¼ cup sifted carob powder
¼ cup milk (soy, dairy, or cashew)
½ teaspoon vanilla
pinch nutmeg or cinnamon (opt.)

Heat butter and sweetener over low heat. When butter is melted, stir in carob powder and milk. Stir until mixture is well blended and begins to thicken. Remove from heat and add vanilla and nutmeg.

Yield: ½ cup, enough to top 8 creme puffs

Thanks to Leslie Curry, Eugene, Oregon for this elegant dessert.

About the Authors

Reggi Norton and Martha Wagner discovered the joy and then the "soy" of cooking some years before they met in Eugene, Oregon. Reggi, granddaughter of an Iowa soybean farmer, is now a natural foods caterer and food coop manager in Takoma Park, Maryland. Martha Wagner, originally from soybean country (Illinois) is a free lance food writer and cooking instructor in Eugene.